THE MAGPIE'S STORY

Marshall Morgan and Scott
Marshall Pickering
3 Beggarwood Lane, Basingstoke, Hants RG23 7LP, UK

Text and illustrations © Nick Butterworth and Mick Inkpen 1988

First published in 1988 by Marshall Morgan and Scott Publications Ltd
Part of the Marshall Pickering Holdings Group
A subsidiary of the Zondervan Corporation
First published in the US by
Zondervan Publishing House, 1415 Lake Drive SE, Grand Rapids, Michigan 49506

British Library CIP Data

Butterworth, Nick
Animal tales: magpie's story.
I. Title II. Inkpen, Mick
823'.914[J] PZ7

ISBN # 0-310-55820-4
Cat # 19091

Printed in Italy by Arnoldo Mondadori Editore

THE MAGPIE'S STORY

JESUS AND ZACCHAEUS

Nick Butterworth and Mick Inkpen

ZONDERVAN

Hello, I'm a magpie. I live in this sycamore tree.

You see the gold ring I'm holding in my beak? I found it. Well, stole it really. I used to have lots of stolen things in my nest. Not any more.

Let me tell you the story. It all began yesterday afternoon…

It's a hot day and I'm sitting out of the sun guarding my stolen treasure.

Suddenly I hear the sound of people laughing.

Down below a large crowd is gathering. That's odd. Usually nothing happens around here in the middle of the afternoon.

The people have lined up along the street. They seem to be waiting for someone. I wonder who it is. He must be important.

Look, even Zacchaeus has come out to see. He's the short, fat man who lives in the big house on the corner. Nobody likes him much. He collects the taxes. They say he's a cheat.

Zacchaeus is too short to see over the crowd. He's trying to push his way to the front. But he's too fat to squeeze through, and the people won't let him past.

They're pretending not to notice him at all. Nobody likes Zacchaeus.

Now he's coming over to my tree. He's climbing up to get a better view! But his short legs won't reach the branches. He's puffing and panting and going red in the face.

Quickly! The important man will be here soon! Go on Zacchaeus, you can do it!

Just in time Zacchaeus scrambles
into the tree. The crowd starts to cheer
and everybody presses forward.

'Hooray, here comes Jesus!'

I can just see his face through the
leaves. But who is Jesus? He doesn't
look important at all. Not like a King,
or a General.

By the look of him he's not even
rich. Just an ordinary man.

Jesus walks up to my tree, stops and looks up through the branches. Perhaps he has spotted my treasure sparkling in the sun.

Does he know I stole it? What does he want?

'Zaccheus, come down,' says Jesus with a laugh. 'I'd like to stay at your house today.'

Zaccheus nearly falls off his branch. What a surprise. Why would anyone want to stay with Zaccheus? Nobody likes Zaccheus.

Zacchaeus climbs down and Jesus says hello. It's very strange. He speaks to Zacchaeus like an old friend.

The crowd doesn't like it at all.

'Why choose Zacchaeus? He's a cheat and a thief!' says one woman.

Now Zacchaeus speaks out loud, for everyone to hear.

'I'll give half of everything I own away,' he says, 'and everyone I've cheated I'll pay back four times over.'

The people are amazed. What has happened to Zacchaeus? He's like a different man.

Since then I've taken back everything
I stole. The things from my nest have
been turning up all over town!

This golden ring is all that's left. I
stole it from the big house on the
corner. Zacchaeus left it on the
window sill.

He'll be pleased to get it back,
I should think.